Unlocking the Secrets of Science

Profiling 20th Century Achievers in Science, Medicine, and Technology

Stephen Wozniak and the Story of Apple Computer

John Riddle and
Jim Whiting

Mitchell Lane
PUBLISHERS

PO Box 619
Bear, Delaware 19701

Unlocking the Secrets of Science

Profiling 20th Century Achievers in Science, Medicine, and Technology

Stephen Wozniak and the Story of Apple Computer

First Printing

Library of Congress Cataloging-in-Publication Data
Riddle, John and Jim Whiting.
   Stephen Wozniak and the story of Apple Computer/John Riddle and Jim Whiting.
     p. cm — (Unlocking the secrets of science)
   Includes bibliographical references and index.
   Summary: A biography covering the personal life and professional career of one of the founders of Apple Computer, Steve Wozniak.
   ISBN 1-58415-109-9
   1. Wozniak, Stephen Gary, 1950—Juvenile literature. 2. Computer science—Biography—Juvenile literature. 3. Apple Computer, Inc.—History—Juvenile literature. 4. Computer industry—United States—History—Juvenile literature. [1. Wozniak, Stephen Gary, 1950- 2. Computer engineers. 3. Apple Computer, Inc.] I. Wozniak, Stephen Gary, 1950- II. Title. III. Series.
QA76.2W69 R53 2001
004.16'092—dc21
   [B]   2001044403

ABOUT THE AUTHOR: John Riddle has been a freelance author and writer for the past 30 years. His byline has appeared in *The Washington Post*; *The New York Times*; *Boston* magazine, and dozens of other publications. He has written for over 100 Web sites and has just completed a biography of Billy Graham for Greenwood Publishing. He is also a sought-after speaker at writing conferences around the country. **Jim Whiting** has been a journalist, writer, editor, and photographer for more than 20 years. In addition to a lengthy stint as publisher of *Northwest Runner* magazine, Mr. Whiting has contributed articles to the *Seattle Times*, *Conde Nast Traveler*, *Newsday*, and *Saturday Evening Post*. He has edited more than 20 titles in the Mitchell Lane Real-Life Reader Biography series and Unlocking the Secrets of Science. He lives in Washington state with his wife and two teenage sons.

PHOTO CREDITS: p. 6 Barbara Marvis; pp. 10, 14 AP Photo; p. 20 Andy Hertzfeld; p. 26 Corbis; p. 30 Corbis-Bettmann; p. 36 AP Photo; p. 39, 40 Al Luckow.

PUBLISHER'S NOTE: In selecting those persons to be profiled in this series, we first attempted to identify the most notable accomplishments of the 20th century in science, medicine, and technology. When we were done, we noted a serious deficiency in the inclusion of women. For the greater part of the 20th century science, medicine, and technology were male-dominated fields. In many cases, the contributions of women went unrecognized. Women have tried for years to be included in these areas, and in many cases, women worked side by side with men who took credit for their ideas and discoveries. Even as we move forward into the 21st century, we find women still sadly underrepresented. It is not an oversight, therefore, that we profiled mostly male achievers. Information simply does not exist to include a fair selection of women.

Contents

The Apple MAC, shown here, evolved in the 1980s and 90s into a graphics machine that is used extensively in the publishing industry.

Chapter 1

An Idea is Born

• •

People don't think twice today about using a personal computer to send e-mail, read, and play games. They also use computers to organize and find information. Many create newsletters using their computer. And computers allow people to access the World Wide Web and the Internet. Children as young as three years old are learning how to use computers.

We take computers for granted now, but until the mid-1970s many people had only seen computers in science fiction movies. One of the most memorable of these cinematic computers, known as HAL, was a main character in the 1968 film *2001: A Space Odyssey*. HAL tried to take over control of the mission into outer space and killed most of the crew before the only surviving member was able to dismantle it.

In the 1970 film *Colossus: The Forbin Project*, a huge computer is constructed to administer the national defense system of the US. But it soon develops a "mind" of its own and begins to communicate with a similar computer in the Soviet Union, the main enemy of the US at that time. Together the two computers try to take over the earth, threatening to destroy the planet if anyone tries to stop them.

But while computers were being presented to the general public in this way, businesses and governments were already starting to use them in a less sinister and much more useful fashion, helping their operations to run more smoothly and efficiently. At first some people were worried that computers might put them out of a job. But soon they learned that computers could help them do their work faster.

While computers helping out in this way are a modern invention, their roots actually go back several thousand years. The earliest ancestor of the computer is the abacus, which performs calculations using beads on a wood and wire framework. It was invented by the Babylonians (some people believe that it was actually the Chinese) between 1000 BC and 500 BC.

The first "modern" device was Charles Babbage's Difference Engine, which he began designing in 1822. He intended for it to help out teams of mathematicians who worked laboriously to create lengthy tables of calculations. Because the people developing these tables performed computations, they were called "computers." This term was used to describe people for more than 100 years. It was finally transferred to the machines themselves because they could perform the necessary functions on their own after being "programmed" by their human operators.

While neither the Difference Engine—which would have been powered by steam—nor Babbage's later Analytical Engine were actually built, he is often regarded as the "father of the computer" because he was the first to produce such designs.

The "children" soon began to appear. One of the most important was Herman Hollerith, whose system of electronically activated punch cards was used to help tabulate the US population in the 1890 census. The company he founded changed its name in 1924 to International Business Machines, which became one of the world's largest and most important electronics companies.

Things really began to heat up just before and during World War II. The Germans invented a complex coding machine called Enigma which they used to send instructions to their ships and armies in the field. They considered the Enigma code to be unbreakable. But the Allies—England and the US—built their own machine to combat Enigma and managed to capture a couple of Enigma devices.

While the war was going on, scientists at the University of Pennsylvania began developing a machine that eventually became known as ENIAC (Electronic Numerical Integrator And Computer), which is often regarded as the first general purpose electronic calculator. About the same time, the Harvard Mark I was introduced.

These early computers were huge contraptions that sometimes required entire buildings to house them. Even though their size began decreasing due to inventions such as the transistor, most were still room-sized. The Mark I, for example, was 50 feet long, eight feet high and weighed five tons.

Not surprisingly, therefore, these huge computers were used almost entirely by businesses, government agencies, and scientific institutions. They had virtually no impact on everyday life. People sent mail using the Post Office. Students doing research for school assignments went to the library and copied notes on index cards. Typists hoped they wouldn't make mistakes while they worked because fixing errors was slow, time-consuming and messy.

But all those things were about to change, and a young man born just south of San Francisco, California would be one of the main reasons.

Steve Wozniak is considered a computer genius. He is credited with inventing the Apple I and II.

Chapter 2

A Genius Is Born

• •

Steve Wozniak was born on August 11, 1950, in San Jose, California. His father Jerry worked as an electrical engineer, while his mother Margaret was a homemaker. Two more children followed, his sister Leslie a little less than two years later and finally Mark, four years after Steve's birth.

When Steve was eight his father got an engineering job at the Lockheed Corporation, which worked on missiles and aerospace technology. The family moved to nearby Sunnyvale, close to Jerry's job.

At an early age, young Steve began to read, and his interests soon began taking a definite turn toward scientific and technological subjects, especially in the fourth grade when he discovered an exciting series.

"I started reading Tom Swift books," he said in an interview with the *San Jose Mercury News*. "They were about this young guy who was an engineer who could design anything, and he owned his own company, and he would entrap aliens, and build submarines, and have projects all over the world. It was just the most intriguing world, like the first TV shows you ever watched."

Tom Swift books weren't the only thing Steve discovered in the fourth grade. He also discovered that he enjoyed math.

So it's probably not a coincidence that he told the *San Jose Mercury News*: "My 4th and 5th grade teacher was a real inspiration to me—she seemed to care about students so much." Her name was Miss Skrak, and she recognized Steve's ability, even though he was a very shy boy and one of the smallest children in his class.

One day Steve's mother visited the class and commented in surprise, "My goodness! Steve's the smallest kid in the class!" According to Martha E. Kendall's book, *Steve Wozniak*, Miss Skark replied, "He may be the smallest in height." Then she tapped her head and added, "But he's the biggest here."

During this time, long distance telephoning was difficult and expensive, so some people, called "hams," used powerful short-wave radios to have conversations with each other and listen to broadcasts from stations around the world. These short-wave radios were much less expensive to operate. When he was in the sixth grade, Steve read a book about a ham radio operator who used his knowledge and skill to help solve a crime. He became interested and soon found out about a class that taught people how to become ham radio operators. Although he was by far the youngest student to take the class, he quickly learned everything he needed to get his ham radio license.

But he wasn't satisfied with just getting his license. By now, he had learned that he loved anything to do with electronics. So he purchased a kit and built his own radio set, both a transmitter and a receiver. Once it was completed, he didn't use it very much, though. Most of the people who were talking back and forth on their radios were adults, and Steve felt too shy to become a part of their conversations.

Building the kit gave Steve the confidence to try other projects, such as a machine that could play tic-tac-toe. His father provided him with advice and leftover electronic components from Lockheed. Because it contained hundreds of parts, his machine turned out to be quite large. For example, the board that held all the electronic circuits measured three feet by four feet.

What Steve didn't realize was that he had built his first computer.

He kept on exploring ideas and information about electronics. Because several of his neighborhood friends shared his interest, they decided to link all their homes with telephone wire and microphones so they could talk to each other.

With all of this experience in electronics, it wasn't surprising that he won the blue ribbon for the best electronics project at the Bay Area Science Fair when he was only 13 years old. All the other blue ribbon winners were in high school. His project was a digital computer that used integrated circuits.

Steve was very excited about his prize, which was a tour of the U.S. Strategic Air Command Facility at Travis Air Force Base near Sacramento, California. He had the chance to see some of the world's most advanced fighter planes and huge cargo aircraft. He even took his first airplane ride. Little did he realize at the time that one day he would become a licensed pilot and fly his own airplanes.

Though this photo was taken well after Steve was out of high school, he actually did not finish his college degree until 1986, nearly 4 years after his son, Jesse John Clark (shown here) was born. Jesse was born in September 1982 during the first UNUSON Festival.

Chapter 3
High School and College Years

• •

By the time Steve enrolled at Homestead High School, electronics was the most important part of his life. His favorite place was the school's electronics lab. Steve was able to enroll in every electronics course that was offered, and always received A's in them. He won the award for being the best electronics student two years in a row. However, Steve soon became bored with the electronic equipment at his high school.

He was very fortunate in one respect: during this period, the mid-1960s, more and more companies dealing in electronics and technology were springing up in the area around San Jose. It soon became known as "Silicon Valley" because much of the new technology used silicon, a chemical element. An important part of sand, silicon is also an excellent insulator and became an integral part of the transistors and computer chips that were so vital to these new companies.

So Homestead's electronics teacher, John McCollum, made arrangements for Steve and another bright student by the name of Allen Baum to go to nearby Sylvania, an electronics company. During their senior year the two boys went to Sylvania after school and programmed computers for them.

Steve did most of his work on an IBM minicomputer. However, it was the size of a normal office desk and therefore "mini" only in relation to the much larger computers then in common use. He became experienced in using IBM punchcards and even more importantly, programming Sylvania's computers using a computer "language" called FORTRAN.

By this time, he had developed a reputation as a brilliant student. Not surprisingly, he was named Homestead's best mathematician in 1966. And not long afterward, he achieved a perfect score of 800 when he took the math portion of the Scholastic Aptitude Test (SAT), one of the main factors that colleges use to determine the students that they will admit.

He was also developing another reputation as well, one that has followed him down to the present day: a prankster.

On more than one occasion, he'd post signs on classroom doors that claimed that the class had been changed to another room. Another favorite prank was to use a pen-sized device that Allen Baum's father had designed. It hopelessly scrambled TV pictures. Steve would sit quietly, turn on his device and try to contain his laughter while his victims kept fiddling with the controls. Then he'd turn it off and let his victims believe that they had fixed the "problem."

But once he almost went too far. He wrapped a device that was supposed to sound like a water faucet dripping in aluminum, stuck some wires on it and put it in a locker at school. It sounded more like the ticking of a clock and resulted in a bomb scare. Because of Steve's reputation, the principal guessed correctly that it was something he'd done and he had the police arrest him. His mother had to come bail him out.

Even though he was suspended from school for a week, the incident didn't affect his graduation from Homestead in 1968.

His parents wanted Steve to attend nearby DeAnza Community College, but he had other plans. He'd visited the University of Colorado the previous fall with a friend and fallen in love with the place after seeing snow for the first time in his life. But it was also very expensive, so he decided to go along with his parents and enroll at DeAnza.

Unfortunately, by the time he'd made this decision all the engineering and math courses he wanted were already filled. So with his family's consent, he changed his plans again and headed for Colorado, where he studied electrical engineering and computer science. He transferred to DeAnza Community College for his sophomore year.

At that point, Steve and his friend Allen Baum decided to take a break from school for a while. They ended up working for a company called Tenet, Incorporated, which was developing a new computer. Steve was responsible for designing and testing a variety of electronic devices. He learned a lot about computer chips and computer designs, and began designing computers in his spare time. However, the company was not successful in selling its new design, and they went out of business in 1970. Steve and his friend found themselves unemployed.

During his unemployment, he used the experience he'd gained to design a primitive computer with the help of another of his electronics buddies, Bill Fernandez. Because of their fondness for a certain kind of soft drink, they called it the Cream Soda Computer. They were so proud of it that they invited a newspaper reporter to come out for a demonstration. But rather than the high speed mathematical calculations it was supposed to generate, all it produced was smoke. The reporter wasn't very impressed and just wrote a couple of paragraphs.

Soon afterward, Steve produced a more successful invention. By now, he was attending the University of California at Berkeley. It was 1971, the height of Vietnam War protests, and Berkeley was one of the most radical campuses in the entire country. It also had an excellent engineering department and was just an hour's drive from Steve's home. Though he didn't participate in the organized protests, Steve did take on one aspect of many Berkeley students: he let his hair grow long and grew a beard.

Not long after beginning his studies at Berkeley, Steve read an article in *Esquire* magazine about a "blue box," a device that allowed its users to mimic telephone company tones so they could literally call anywhere in the world without being billed. The article presented the box as fiction, but Steve believed that he could build one. He was right. The device was so successful that Steve was able to call the Vatican City and asked to speak to the Pope. The person who answered the phone informed him that the leader of the Catholic Church was asleep but would wake him up. Steve hung up.

Steve decided he should manufacture and sell his new blue box. He went to visit his friend, Steve Jobs. Jobs was still attending Homestead high school. Even though Steve Wozniak was five years older than the other Steve, Jobs was much more outgoing. So their partnership worked like this: Steve Wozniak would build the blue boxes, Steve Jobs would sell them. The two would split the profits.

Though their venture worked for a little while, both soon moved on to other things. Steve Jobs graduated from high school and began attending Reed College in Portland, Oregon. And Steve Wozniak, needing money to pay for his college education, began working for a company called Electroglas, testing electronic components.

A few years later they would re-unite. And this time their partnership would create a profound revolution in the way that people conducted their daily lives.

Steve, right, is shown here with his friend, Joey Slotnick.

Chapter 4

A Desire for Something More

● ●

Steve's old high school friend Allen Baum was working at Hewlett-Packard, one of the leading electronics companies in Silicon Valley at the time. Not long after Steve began working at Electroglas, Baum arranged a job interview for him at Hewlett-Packard. Impressed with his obvious electronics ability, H-P (as the company was known for short) quickly offered him a job as an associate engineer in their calculator division even though he didn't have a college degree. Shortly, he was promoted to full engineer.

H-P was an ideal place for Steve to work. Unlike many American companies at that time, H-P allowed its employees to wear pretty much anything they cared to while they worked. They also encouraged "flex time," allowing employees to work whatever hours they preferred as long as they fulfilled their obligations. Perhaps most importantly for Steve's future, they allowed their employees to pursue outside interests on the company premises, as long as it was past their normal working hours.

It was during his days at Hewlett-Packard that Steve acquired his various nicknames such as "The Woz," "The Wizard of Woz," or simply "Woz," which is how he is usually addressed even today.

In this environment, he devoted all his energy to his interests in electronics. Though he'd originally started working to earn money for college, he didn't return right away. Instead, he spent a lot of time working with electronic chips for calculators. Taking advantage of H-P's policy allowing their employees to work on personal projects at night using company equipment, Steve began writing programs for computer games that created the first graphics ever used on a computer.

Meanwhile, Jobs had drifted back into Silicon Valley. After dropping out of college, he traveled to India and later worked on a communal farm in Oregon. At this time, he was working at nearby Atari, the company that began the video arcade phenomenon with its game Pong. The two Steves often got together, with Jobs showing Woz some of the new games that were being designed, and they'd play them for hours on end.

One day, Jobs told Woz about a challenge: Atari wanted a new computer game, one that used far fewer than the 150 or more computer chips that were common in most games as a way to save money. But it had to be completed in four days. Woz did most of the technical work, got little sleep, but met both challenges: the game he designed, called Breakout, used just 43 chips. And he finished it in the allotted four days. Jobs presented the game to Atari.

Both Woz and Jobs were also members of the Homebrew Computer Club, a group of young computer engineers who enjoyed getting together to exchange ideas and just hang out with each other because of their common passion for electronics.

Woz had been working on a circuit board designed to run a new, relatively inexpensive microprocessor. He hooked it up to a television, power supply, and keyboard. He called the circuit board itself the computer and took it to a Homebrew Club meeting. It was a momentous event, part of a process that had been going on for a long time.

"Designing computers, which had become the love of my life, was like solving puzzles," Woz told the *San Jose Mercury News*. "I tried to get better and better and better. If I designed a computer with 200 chips, I [then] tried to design it with 150. And then I would try to design it with 100. I just tried to find every trick I could in life to design things real tiny.

"The first Apple was just a culmination of my whole life. My whole life had been designing computers I could never build. And all of a sudden I discovered that the prices of some parts called 'microprocessors' and 'memory chips' had gotten so low that I could actually afford, with maybe a month's salary (if I saved for a little while) to design and build my own computer."

At that time, almost all computers were still large and expensive, intended for business use. The only ones available for home use were in kit form, meaning that only experts in electronics could even assemble them. And they were also very difficult to understand and to use.

"These things were kind of strange," he said of those early kits, "because I'm a normal person who believes in the very middle road and just having a normal life and doing what normal people do. I had a TV set and a typewriter and that made me think a computer should be laid out like a typewriter with a video screen. I'd learned enough about circuitry in high school electronics to know how to drive a TV and get it to draw—shapes of characters and things. So it's like all these influences came together and out came a product that I knew would be easy to use the way I liked to use a computer at my job at Hewlett Packard, which was to solve engineering problems, and occasionally to solve a puzzle, and also to play games."

Steve Jobs was impressed with Woz's new creation and as they'd done earlier with the blue boxes, thought that they could make some money selling them. Jobs' first idea was to make 50 bare circuit boards, which would cost a little over $1,000 because they cost about $20 each to produce. Then they'd turn around and sell them for $40 to people like themselves, people who enjoyed computers as a hobby. Woz wasn't so sure. He thought they'd have trouble selling all 50. Besides, he still enjoyed his job at Hewlett-Packard, and liked creating new electronic equipment.

Even though he had created the circuit board on his own time, he had used the facilities at H-P to build it. In addition, it would be easier for H-P to manufacture and sell the circuit boards than it would be for the two young men. So he showed his design to the company's legal department, which in turn asked every division at H-P if they were interested in taking it over. But no one at H-P was interested in making personal computers, so a few days later the company released any legal interest in the design. It now belonged completely to Woz. And he agreed to form a company with Jobs.

Their first decision was to come up with a name for their new company. The name "Apple" came from Jobs, possibly because he'd worked in an apple orchard. It was a simple name, which seemed appropriate for their crude computer. On April Fool's Day, 1976, Apple Computer officially came into being. Woz was 26 and Jobs was 21.

Now that they had a name for their company, they needed to raise money. Jobs sold his Volkswagen van and

Woz sold his programmable calculator. That gave them a total of $1,350. Next, they needed to find a place to set up their business, with enough room to allow them to build their new circuit boards. They did the design work in Steve Jobs' bedroom and the assembly work in his garage.

About a month after they had officially opened their doors they received their first big order. A man named Paul Terrell owned a retail computer store called The Byte Shop. After Jobs demonstrated their computer for him at a meeting of the Homebrew Club, Terrell placed an order with Apple Computer for 100 Apple I computers, rather than just the bare circuit boards, and offered to pay $500 for each one.

That created two problems for the new company. One was financial. They had almost no cash, yet they needed money to buy all the additional parts they'd need to fill the Byte Shop order. But Jobs was able to borrow $5,000 from friends and, even better, talked a local electronics supplier into giving them $15,000 worth of parts on credit. They had 30 days to pay the supplier back.

In addition, the two young men couldn't do all the work themselves. Within a few days they had contacted a friend of Jobs who was still working at Atari. Their friend agreed that if they supplied the plans, he would lay out the printed circuit board. Other friends pitched in and they made the completed delivery just before they had to pay back the $15,000 they'd taken out on credit.

"The Byte Shop order was the biggest single episode in the company's history," Woz said in Owen Linzmayer's *Apple Confidential.* "Nothing in subsequent years was so great and so unexpected. It was not what we had intended to do."

Steve Jobs is the marketing genius behind Apple Computer. The company floun-dered without his help in the early 1990s, but Steve returned the company to profitability when he returned in 1997.

Chapter 5

The Apple Gets Bigger

● ●

Even though they enjoyed modest success with their first order, clearing about $8,000, and sold additional units to hobbyists and experts in electronics, Apple Computer Company was not making enough money for Steve Wozniak to make a salary yet. So he still kept working at Hewlett-Packard. But he continued working and experimenting with new computer designs. In spite of its good qualities, the Apple I lacked many essentials such as a keyboard and case. It also had to be assembled by the purchaser.

Jobs, meanwhile, was working on bigger plans for their company, but he knew he had to come up with a plan to get a lot more money. Through his contacts at Atari, he had met a man named Mike Markkula, a successful businessman who had retired at the age of 33 after making his fortune with several other computer companies.

Markkula saw a lot of potential in Apple Computer. Within a few weeks he had written a business plan for Apple, one that had a goal of increasing sales to $500 million within 10 years. He obtained a $250,000 line of credit and even invested $90,000 of his own money in the company. And he convinced Woz to leave H-P and devote full time to the new company.

Apple Computer became a corporation in January of 1977, and listed Steve Wozniak, Steve Jobs, and Mike Markkula as the owners. They immediately began putting the new business plan that Markkula had created into action. By now Apple Computer had already outgrown Steve Jobs' garage, so the company moved into an office building in Cupertino and hired several new employees. Several were young men whom Woz had known in the electronics lab at Homestead High School. All were very bright and very excited to be working at their new company.

Everyone agreed that Apple Computer needed a bold logo that would show the world what they were all about. Rob Janov, the art director at the advertising and public relations agency of Regis McKenna, created the distinctive design with six bright horizontal bands of color that Apple still uses.

"I wanted to simplify the shape of an apple, and by taking a bite—a byte, right?—out of the side, it prevented the apple from looking like a cherry tomato," explains Janov in *Apple Confidential*. "Byte" is a computer term that refers to the units of memory contained on a chip.

But Apple was much more than a colorful logo and a few bright electronics technicians. Woz had already completed the design of his next computer, what became known as the Apple II. It featured a keyboard, color graphics, its own power supply, and what at that time was a large memory capacity. Everything was enclosed in a plastic case. Even more important, at $1,298 it was affordable for many people. And purchasers didn't need to be computer experts to use it.

In April, 1977 the Apple II made its debut at the West Coast Computer Faire and made a strong impression. Once the trade show was over, Apple Computer began a national ad campaign, placing ads in magazines read by everyday people. One of their slogans was "Byte into an Apple," and it gave consumers an interest in what they had to offer. Within a few months, sales mushroomed.

By the end of their first year, Apple Computer had achieved $774,000 in sales and earned a profit of $42,000. By the following year's Consumer Electronics Show in Las Vegas, Nevada, Apple was ready to show off more improvements that Woz had designed for the Apple II. One was an interface card that would allow Apple computers to be hooked up to printers. Woz had also created a disk drive that replaced earlier cassette tapes and made it far easier and faster to find and read information. Because the Apple II was becoming even simpler to operate, a new phrase came into being: "user-friendly."

At that time, there were only two other ready-to-use personal computers being sold, one from Radio Shack, and one from Commodore. But neither had a disk drive, so most people who decided to buy a computer bought the new Apple II. By the end of 1978, Apple Computer was proclaimed one of the fastest growing companies in America.

Within three years, the company had made more than three hundred million dollars and it took the next step: it went public. That meant that anyone could buy shares of Apple Computer stock. On the first day that stock was available, so many people wanted to buy it that the price was pushed higher and higher. Because Woz and Jobs owned so many shares already, they suddenly found themselves very wealthy men. Steve Wozniak, the young man who had to sell his programmable calculator just four years earlier to help raise the $1,350 to put his company in business, was now a millionaire many times over.

From left to right: Steve Jobs, John Sculley, and Steve Wozniak unveil the new Apple computer.

Chapter 6
Steve Has a Wake-up Call

• •

All of this phenomenal growth came with a price. Apple Computer had become a large corporation with many employees. It became harder and harder for Woz to have a personal relationship with everyone who worked there. And by this time Apple Computer had become so famous that Woz found himself spending much of his time giving speeches to civic and educational groups. It left him little time to design new computers and applications, and this began to frustrate him.

"My whole life, I did not want to be a company runner. I just wanted to be a good engineer, wanted to write programs, design computers," he told *the San Jose Mercury News.*

Soon he began spending time away from Apple in search of other interests. Perhaps because of the trip to Travis Air Force Base he'd won from the science fair more than 10 years earlier, one of those interests was taking flying lessons. Within a short time he earned his pilot's license and purchased his own airplane, a single-engine, 300-horsepower Beechcraft Bonanza.

On February 7, 1981, Woz was getting ready to fly his fiancée, Candi Clark—who was an accountant at Apple Computer—and her brother and his girlfriend to San Diego. Taxiing down the runway, he lost control of his airplane, which veered off into the tall grass. Steve never remembered exactly what happened. Doctors said that he was suffering from "anterograde amnesia," something that often happens to people who are in car crashes.

When Steve realized that he could have died in the crash, he began thinking about how he was spending his life. Soon afterward he married Candi and decided to leave Apple for a while to go back to college and finish his degree. He re-enrolled at the University of California at Berkeley using the name of Rocky Raccoon Clark. Because he was already famous and did not want to be recognized, he used a fictitious name. Always the prankster, he simply combined his dog's name with his new wife's maiden name.

Steve considered himself to be just another regular student. He carried a backpack, attended classes and studied all hours of the night. He was especially intrigued by a psychology course. Steve discovered that the human brain and computers were very similar. Still a few courses short of earning his degree, Steve left Berkeley after a year.

He formed a corporation called "UNUSON" ("Unite Us In Song") that sponsored two three-day rock music and technology events called the "US Festival." The first one was held during Labor Day weekend in 1982, and the second one in 1983. Even though he lost an estimated $20 million on the two concerts, he had a good time. One of the main reasons was that his first child, a son named Jesse, was born the day before the festival started and Woz proudly introduced him on national TV. Another was that he used new technology to broadcast the festival to the Soviet Union—at that time the main enemy of the US in what was known as the Cold War—and in turn show Soviet bands on a giant screen at the US Festival.

Soon afterward, he decided to go back to Apple.

But it was far from the same company that he had founded six years earlier. After several years when Apple Computer could do no wrong, several problems were emerging. One was the growth of other computer companies, one of whom was IBM. These companies were taking sales away from Apple. Another was that the Apple III, the next computer in their line, had several problems and had to be recalled. Still another was that Apple Computer Corporation, which now had several divisions, had feuds within their own divisions.

Steve Jobs recruited the president of Pepsi-Cola, John Sculley, to be the new president of Apple Computer. He was confident that Sculley could solve all of their problems and help them concentrate on selling computers. But Jobs himself was the source of some of the problems. He was known to be very harsh and abrasive in dealing with other people. It was difficult to work in this environment with so much stress.

So when Woz returned to work at Apple, in the Apple II department, people were glad to see him come back because they found him easy to work with and he was always joking around. Steve thought morale at the company was important, and he was always doing things to make people happy.

Back at work again, Steve was ready to tackle a new idea. When he saw the first computer mouse at a demonstration at the Palo Alto Research Center he wanted to find a way to make it work with Apple's computers. It became known as the Lisa project, and everyone was excited at the possibilities. The new Lisa computer would have many improvements over the Apple II. But it was enormously expensive and did not sell well. During that time, the feuding among several different departments at Apple grew even worse.

That didn't stop Apple Computer from launching an "Apple II Forever" conference in San Francisco in 1984. Over 2,000 computer dealers from around the country ordered over 50,000 Apple II computers. That helped boost sales of the Apple II computer to over two million units.

A few months later, Apple Computer introduced the Macintosh. With their ad campaign that told people to "Test Drive a Macintosh," they offered to let people take home a computer for 24 hours to see how they liked it. Some two hundred thousand people took them up on their offer, and people were soon finding out how easy and fun the Macintosh was to use and own.

But the relationship between Apple's two founders was anything but "easy and fun."

The two men were very different in their personalities and in their approach to business. In the beginning, it had seemed an ideal arrangement: Woz's engineering genius matched with Jobs' determination and business sense.

By this time, Jobs was solidly backing the new Macintosh—even to the point of giving favorable treatment to the employees who were working on it—and Woz was hurt that he seemed to be virtually ignoring the Apple II, the company's bread and butter machine.

He also heard that Jobs had apparently cheated him when they had designed the Breakout game a decade earlier. Another employee told Woz that Jobs had been paid $5000 for the game, not $700 as Jobs had told him.

To this day, no one is entirely certain of the truth. Woz says that memories do fade with time and this employee might not have remembered the exact amount that Jobs was given. In any event, it was a long time ago, and Woz has moved past it.

"It wasn't the money that bothered Woz," says Owen Linzmayer in *Apple Confidential*. "Had Jobs asked, Wozniak would have done the project for free because he was turned on by such technological challenges. What hurt was being misled by his friend."

And Woz added, "Steve Jobs will use anybody to his own advantage. He will say one thing and anybody who heard it would think that he was saying 'Maybe yes' or 'Maybe no.' You could never tell what he was thinking."

In short, Steve Wozniak had one idea for running the company, and Steve Jobs had another. In February of 1985, Steve Wozniak left the company again, this time for good.

Steve enrolled at Cal Berkeley under the name of Rocky Raccoon Clark. He finally received his engineering degree in 1986, 18 years after he first enrolled in college at the University of Colorado. In those 18 years, he helped build Apple Computer.

Chapter 7
Life After Apple

• •

Just over a year later, Woz finally received his engineering degree from Cal Berkeley. The San Francisco Chronicle called him "the student most likely to have already succeeded."

He was invited to be the commencement speaker at the graduation ceremonies, and everyone laughed when he began his address with a joke: "I'm glad to have a degree so I can go out and get a good-paying job."

Soon afterward, he started a company called CL-9—which stood for "Cloud Nine"—with a former Apple engineer named Joe Ennis. The company was intended to develop an infrared remote control that would work with any home entertainment system. Steve saw many possibilities with their new company, and was excited to be working on a new project once again.

Because of Steve's celebrity status, the media thought when he left Apple that something was wrong. He kept trying to convince everyone that he had no problems with Apple's management. He told everyone he was only interested in creating a new electronic device.

Steve invested a half a million dollars in his new company. He also had no trouble getting other investors because of his reputation. So CL-9 set up an office in a shopping center located in Los Gatos.

He was back in the swing of things, once again creating and experimenting with new electronic devices. But he soon ran into a problem. He had asked a company called Frog Design to design the casing for their new electronic device, which they were calling CORE. But since Frog Design also did work for Apple Computer, Steve Jobs stepped in and told Frog Design not to work with CL-9, claiming that Woz's new company was competing with Apple. Since Woz had a letter from the head of the Apple II division saying specifically that he wasn't competing, he was hurt. Because of this and several other disagreements with Jobs, Woz rarely saw his former partner again.

By this time, Jobs was having his own troubles at Apple Computer. He and CEO John Sculley were always disagreeing. A short time later Jobs left the company and started his own company called NeXT Computers. He tried to take some of Apple's engineers with him, but Apple sued and they settled out of court. As part of the settlement Jobs was not able to hire any Apple personnel for at least three years.

As things turned out, CL-9 didn't stay in business very long. The company wasn't able to produce its remote devices as quickly as Woz had hoped it could. He was spending too much time giving speeches and making public appearances. He also enjoyed being with his children. Soon he found out that RCA and several Japanese companies had already introduced similar remote control devices. All these factors resulted in his decision to close the company, and he sold the technology in 1989.

Steve then opened a personal office in Los Gatos with his friend Jim Valentine. He used the name UNUSON from his music festivals several years earlier, and devoted considerable time to giving away money. Some of the projects he supported included the Tech Museum of Innovation in San Jose, the Children's Discovery Museum, and the San Jose-Cleveland Ballet. Steve was a generous man, and didn't mind sharing his wealth with other people.

Steve is a generous man and he works tirelessly to help other people.

Steve loves to play all sorts of games and he has a large game room in his home.

Chapter 8
Woz Today

• •

T hese days Steve Wozniak keeps very busy, although he leads a somewhat private life.

He is now married to his third wife, Suzanne Mulkern. They were married in 1990, and between them they have six kids—three of Steve's from his marriage to Candi Clark and three from Suzanne's first marriage. They actually knew each other in junior high, and Suzanne jokes in *People* magazine that "He was the nerd, I was the cheerleader."

Woz still has an office where he works on various projects to give back to society. He spends a lot of time on his own computers. And starting back in 1991 when his son Jesse discovered how wonderful computers were, he began teaching his son and other children how to use them in after-school computer classes.

He continues to do this, and has also purchased computers and computer labs for local schools. He focuses on students in the fourth and fifth grades in elementary schools, explaining that those years were the most important to him when he was in school. He understands how curious students at that age really are. He knows he can make a difference in his students' lives, and he wants to do whatever he can to help them.

Steve's philosophy about education is very simple. He believes in a "hands-on" learning style. In other words, if young students are given the chance to hold a computer, to look inside and see how it works, they will do better in school and in life. So he won't hesitate to take a computer apart in front of his students just to show them what the insides look like. Most people have never seen the inside of a computer, and many are afraid to take them apart and look inside.

He always tells students that if they have a passion for learning and a passion for computers that they should keep studying. Study everything about computers you can find. Learn how to run a computer program. Learn how to write a computer program. Practice everyday and when you get bored with something, find something new that excites you. That way you will always be learning, and will always be improving your life. It doesn't matter if a student never ends up working with computers as a career. By learning and studying about computers in school, they will be building a better life for themselves.

Although he cares very much about his subject, The Woz isn't your typical classroom teacher. In The Tech Museum of Innovation's online site, Steve talks about one of his favorite pranks.

"How would you like a Mac of your own?" he asked his students one day. They all knew that "Mac" is what Macintosh owners call their computers.

Of course every hand in the room went up. So he told them that the next time they came to class, he would give them their own Macs. Sure enough, when they arrived for their next lesson, Macintosh computers were prominently displayed. Steve had them come into his classroom, gave them an hour and a half lesson with everyone listening closely to what he said, and finished up with a short quiz.

"As soon as you finish your tests, go out and pick up your Macs," he told them.

The eager students hurried out of the classroom after finishing their work and found their Macs waiting. They were Macs, all right—Big Macs from a nearby McDonald's restaurant.

While he still cares deeply about the company he founded, he's disappointed with the direction that the Apple Computer Corporation decided to take. In a 1996 article in *Newsweek* magazine, he wrote, "Our first computers were born not out of greed or ego but in the revolutionary spirit of helping common people. Our vision was that people would find computers useful at home, for 'people things' like balancing checkbooks, keeping address lists and typing letters.

"But after a while, Apple lost touch with its core market. We decided to go after small business owners who could use a spreadsheet, and designed a computer especially for them, the Apple III. With IBM nipping at our heels, every project and ad for three years was for the Apple III and not for the largest-selling computer worldwide, the Apple II.

"It was the Macintosh, though, that became our flagship machine and spoke to the masses. It carried a message that you didn't have to think linearly and you didn't have to keep computer gibberish in your head. The Mac was the first personal computer with a mouse and menus and windows, not to mention built-in networking and LaserWriters. Files could even be named as humans would name them. We revived the dream of people mastering technology.

"The computer was never the problem. The company's strategy was. Apple saw itself as a hardware company; in order to protect our hardware profits, we didn't license our operating system. We had the most beautiful operating system, but to get it you had to buy our hardware at twice the price. That was a mistake. What we should have done was calculate an appropriate price to license the operating system."

These days Steve Wozniak has been inducted into the Inventor's Hall of Fame, he is still teaching computer classes in his local schools, and he has his own Web site. If you go to http://www.woz.org you will see a very exciting and interesting Web site. You can discover more information about his life and how he spent some of his time in school.

Several years ago, Woz told Guy Kawasaki in an interview published in *Hindsights-The Wisdom and Breakthroughs of Remarkable People* that "In the sixth grade, I decided I was going to be an engineer, and then I was going to be an elementary school teacher. That's what I've done. I could have had a lot of fun in Apple and been involved in some great things going on in the world, but I really feel better about what I am doing.

"I want to be remembered as a good computer designer who designed things with very few parts and wrote code that was very amazing and tricky and ingenious. I want to be remembered as a good father who cared about children. Every step of my life has been incredible. I have a lot of freedom. I get to do a lot of traveling and see a lot of things. I've got wonderful children. Nobody could have a life better than mine."

Steve Wozniak Chronology

- 1950, born on August 11
- 1968, graduates from Homestead High School and attends University of Colorado
- 1969, attends DeAnza College
- 1971, attends University of California at Berkeley
- 1973, works for Hewlett-Packard
- 1976, marries Alice Robertson
- 1976, founds Apple Computer with Steve Jobs
- 1977, introduces Apple II computer
- 1981, marries Candi Clark
- 1982, sponsors first US Festival, three-day concert near San Bernardino, California
- 1985, leaves Apple Computer
- 1985, receives National Medal of Technology from President Ronald Reagan.
- 1986, receives Bachelor of Science degree from University of California, Berkeley
- 1990, marries third wife, Suzanne Mulkern
- 1992, begins teaching grade school students about math and computers
- 2001, still teaches computer classes at local schools

Computer Timeline

- **1000-500 BC** — Babylonians (some historians believe it was the Chinese) invent the abacus, the forerunner of the computer.
- **1500s** - Leonardo da Vinci sketches design for mechanical calculator
- **1822**: Charles Babbage begins designing his Difference Engine
- **1842**: Ada Lovelace becomes first computer programmer
- **1925**: Vannevar Bush of the Massachusetts Institute of Technology invents the differential analyzer
- **1940**: George Steblitz transmits mathematical problem from Dartmouth College to his Complex Number Calculator in New York, the first example of a network
- **1947**: transistor is invented
- **1948**: Creation of UNIVAC, the first commercial computer
- **1952**: CBS-TV uses UNIVAC computer to predict outcome of presidential election

- **1954**: Texas Instruments announces start of commercial production of silicon transistors
- **1958**: Texas Instruments builds first integrated circuit
- **1963**: Douglas Englebart patents mouse pointing device for computers
- **1972**: Bill Gates and Paul Allen form Traf-O-Data company, which is renamed Microsoft three years later
- **1976**: Steve Jobs and Steve Wozniak form Apple Computer Company on April Fool's Day
- **1982**: Time magazine names the computer its "Man of the Year"
- **1990**: Apple Computer's AppleLink - Personal Edition is renamed America Online
- **Late 1990s**: Bill Gates of Microsoft Corporation becomes world's richest man

Further Reading

Books for children and young adults:

Blow, Lisa. *How to Use Computers*. Que Publishing Company, 1998.

Carlton, Jim. *Apple: The Inside Story of Intrigue, Egomania, and Business Blunders*. New York: Random House, 1997.

Gookin, Dan. *PCs for Dummies*. Hungry Minds, Inc., 1999.

Kendall, Martha. *Steve Wozniak: Inventor of the Apple Computer*. Los Gatos, CA: Highland Books, 2000.

Linzmayer, Owen W. *Apple Confidential*. San Francisco, CA: No Starch Press, 1999.

Stephens, Margaret. *Computers for Beginners*. EDC Publications, 1998.

White, Ron. *How Computers Work : Millennium Edition* Que Publishers, 1999.

On the Web:

http://www.landsnail.com/apple/1990s.html

http://www.thetech.org/people/interviews/woz.html

http://jinx.umsl.edu/~sbmeade/macway/woz.html

http://www.ruku.com/wozniak.html

http://www.usnews.com/usnews/issue/991227/wozniak.html

http://www.execpc.com/~shepler/cringely.html

http://www.woz.org

Glossary of Terms

BASIC – Beginner's All-Purpose Symbolic Instruction Code. This computer code was popular with computers made in the 1970s and 1980s.

Bit –abbreviation for binary digit. Computers keep track of information using data in the form of bits.

Breadboard –computer board that is used to test new electronic components. People who create new computer designs use a breadboard that can be assembled and disassembled easily.

Byte – unit of memory contained on a chip, consisting of eight bits of information. In computer programming, a byte can be a letter, single digit number, a single space or a symbol.

CD-ROM –flat round disk also known as a CD. It can store huge amounts of information; more than a floppy disk can. Most computers today come with CD-ROM drives.

Chip –very small piece of silicon used to store information in computers.

Circuit –journey that electricity follows. It requires an electrical source and other electronic components, including conductors and transistors.

Circuit Board –piece of plastic or fiberglass that contains metal strips to link a variety of electronic components.

Disk Drive – device used to read a floppy disk or a CD-ROM.

Electrical Engineer – person who learns about electrical theory and can use that knowledge to build and design computers and other electrical devices.

Electronics – any study dealing with physics and the flow of electrons.

FORTRAN – computer language used by computer programmers working in engineering and science.

Hard Drive –section of a computer that stores and processes information.

Hardware – mechanical and electronic parts of a computer system, including keyboard, monitor, disk drives, etc.

Infrared Remote Controller – portable electronic device that sends instructions to nearby electronic equipment.

Mainframe – primary type of computers before personal computers were invented, sometimes as large as a room.

Resistor – component in an electrical circuit that reduces the flow of current in that circuit.

Silicon – material found in sand that acts as an insulator when used as part of an electronic component.

Software – computer programs that tell computers what to do.

Transistor – component in a computer chip that controls the electrical flow.

Transmitter – electronic device that sends information over the airways.

Index